WORLD IN VIEW
MIDDLE EAST
Ian A. Morrison

STECK-VAUGHN
LIBRARY
Austin, Texas

© **Copyright 1991, text, Steck-Vaughn Company.**

Library of Congress Cataloging-in-Publication Data

Morrison, Ian A.
    Middle East / Ian A. Morrison.
        p.   cm.—(World in view)
    Includes index.
    Summary: A general survey of the Middle East with information
on its geography, languages, religions, history, occupations,
family life, cities, education, food, and legacies.
    ISBN 0-8114-2440-5
    1. Middle East—Juvenile literature. [1. Middle East.]
I. Title. II. Series.
DS44.M66   1991
956—dc20   90-24433
                               CIP AC

Cover: *The Stock Exchange in Kuwait.*
Title page: *A popular idea of the Middle East*

Designed by Julian Holland Publishing Ltd

Typeset by Multifacit Graphics, Keyport, NJ
Printed and bound in the United States
by Lake Book, Melrose Park, IL
1 2 3 4 5 6 7 8 9 0 LB 95 94 93 92 91

Photographic credits:
Cover: © James Willis/TSW-Click/Chicago Ltd.
All photographs by Ian A. Morrison except pages 11, 32, 88
where photos are by T. Pedder

Contents

MIDDLE EAST

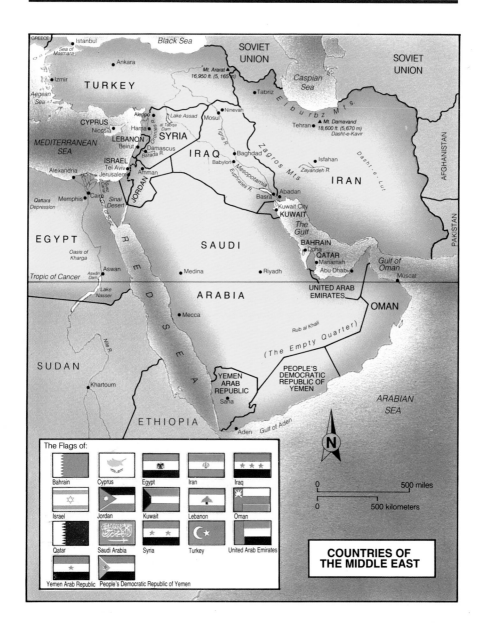

COUNTRIES OF
THE MIDDLE EAST

1 Where Continents Meet

The "Middle East" is a strange name to use for an area. It was invented by Europeans, to mean somewhere between Europe and the countries of eastern Asia, which are known as the Far East. Although the people who live in the Middle East did not give it that name themselves, they have found it convenient to use it in the same way that people use the Midwest in America. In Arabic it is called *Sharq al Awsat* or East-the-Middle, because there is such variety to the region that it is difficult to find any other single term to describe all the differences there are.

Many people who have not been there imagine that all of the Middle East looks alike. They think

Not all the deserts of the Middle East are sandy. The vegetation stops and the glare of the salt flats begins at the edge of the Dasht e Kavir, *the Great Salt Desert of central Iran.*

5

Fact Box

★ The Middle East covers an area of 2.5 million square miles (6.5 million square kilometers). This is two-thirds the size of the United States.

★ The Nile River, which runs through Egypt, is the longest river in the world at 4,160 miles (6,695 kilometers).

★ The Dead Sea, a large lake on the border between Israel and Jordan, is 1,279 feet (390 meters) below sea level. It is the lowest point on land in the world.

★ The population of the Middle East is about 165 million.

★ There is much empty land, for example in Saudi Arabia, which is about one-third the size of the United States. However, its population is only about 12 million, which is approximately the size of metropolitan Los Angeles.

★ Most of the land is scrub, desert, or mountains and only about five percent of the land can be used to grow crops.

★ Some of the Middle East's deserts are covered in sand dunes more than 980 feet (300 meters) high.

★ The United Arab Emirates is one of the richest countries in the world. The two Yemen republics are among the poorest.

★ The Middle East is the world's largest producer of oil.

★ The countries of the Middle East produce about 10 million barrels of oil each day.

★ Saudi Arabia has the largest supplies of oil and first produced oil for industry in 1938.

of it as one huge, sun-scorched, sandy desert, where oil-rich Arabs follow the religion of Islam. However, not everybody in the Middle East is a Muslim, which is what a follower of Islam is called, and many languages besides Arabic are spoken. Nor are the people all rich. Some are very poor. It is true that there are deserts, but there are also snow-covered mountains and some of the most productive lowland farms in the world.

Three influences
It is not really surprising to find such a mixture of peoples and landscapes there. The Middle East lies at a crossroads where three continents meet, with Asia, Africa, and Europe each influencing its geography and history. The results have often been unique, so that despite its variety the Middle East may be thought of as a region in its own right. The Middle East is not Asia, Africa, or Europe, although it has parts like each of them.

The land and sea routes radiating from the Middle East have not only carried ideas into the area, they have also carried ideas out. Today, the rest of the world is very aware of the importance of the Middle East, because so much of the Earth's oil reserves lie there. However, the influence of the Middle East on the rest of the world is nothing new. It goes back thousands of years before oil became such an important source of energy.

Early farming
For example, it is difficult to imagine a world without farming, where all food had to be gathered from the wild or hunted as it was in prehistoric days. Different kinds of farming

7

The farmers of the Middle East soon learned how to make the best use of available water. Noria is the name for the great irrigation wheels used at Hama in western Syria. In the past, this kind of device was also used in North Africa and as far afield as Spain, where it was introduced by the Muslim conquerors in the eighth, century.

developed in various parts of the world. The type most familiar to North Americans, Europeans, and Australians grew out of the farming first practiced by Middle Easterners nearly 10,000 years ago. The ancestors of familiar farm animals, such as sheep and goats, roamed wild in the hills of the Middle East until they were tamed and domesticated. There too grew wild grasses from which crops such as wheat and barley evolved.

The Middle East was one of the first places in the world to have cities. It was also the source of three of the great religions of the world: Judaism, Christianity, and Islam. The influence of the Middle East on cultures in other parts of the world is a broad one. It encompasses science, the arts, many games that we play, and the basis of a surprising number of the words used by other nationalities.

Countries of the Middle East

So which countries actually make up the Middle East? In many respects, the Arabian Peninsula is the center. Mecca, the holiest city of Islam, is there. The old name "Arabia" used to describe the whole peninsula, but this area is now split among several states. By far the largest of these is called Saudi Arabia, after its ruling family the Sauds. Saudi Arabia is roughly the size of Western Europe, but it is a desert land with only about 11.5 million people. However, it does hold a large proportion of the world's remaining oil, as does the little state of Kuwait at the head of the Arabian Gulf. The other Arab states on the Gulf are also small. They are Bahrain, Qatar, and the

This is not a natural hill, but Tel Braq, a huge artificial mound gradually built up over thousands of years from the remains of a city of mud-brick houses. Tel Braq is in northern Syria but there are many tell mounds in the Middle East that show how ancient the tradition of city building is in the region.

Population Figures: in millions

Turkey	51.55
Egypt	49.9
Iran	48.0
Iraq	16.1
Saudi Arabia	11.6
Syria	10.7
Yemen AR	9.2
Israel	4.4
Jordan	2.7
Lebanon	2.7
Yemen PDR	2.4
Kuwait	2.0
UA Emirates	1.6
Oman	1.3
Cyprus	0.7
Bahrain	0.4
Qatar	0.3

United Arab Emirates. The Emirates are really tiny, except for Abu Dhabi. They are called Dubai, Sharjah, Umm al-Qaiwain, Ras al-Khaimah, Fujairah, and Ajman. The amount of oil the Emirates produce makes them some of the richest states in the world. The average income for each person living there is well above that of Switzerland, Europe's richest country, and nearly twice that of the United States. Oman faces out from the Arabian Peninsula toward the Indian Ocean, and the two Yemen states at the entrance to the Red Sea are the Yemen Arab Republic (Yemen AR) and the People's Democratic Republic of Yemen (South Yemen PDR). The Yemens are among the poorest countries in the world; their people average only about two percent of the income of those in the Emirates.

Arabic-speaking countries

Arabic is the main language throughout the Arabian Peninsula, and in Iraq, Syria, and Jordan to the north. Hebrew is the official language of Israel, but many people there are Arabic speakers. To the west, Arabic is dominant in Egypt, Libya, and the other North African states beyond, to Morocco. The Arabic-speaking countries thus stretch for over 3,700 miles (6,000 kilometers), from the Atlantic to the Indian Ocean, and Arabic is a shared language over an area as big as the United States. However, two of the largest states in the Middle East have quite different kinds of languages. These are Turkey, with its own language, Turkish, and Iran, where Persian (Farsi) is spoken.

Many of the people in the newly oil-rich countries are able to build themselves very beautiful new homes. Although this house is very modern, many traditional features are still used.

In the heat of the Middle East, the shady side of the street is always the place for discussions, no matter which country you are in.

All of the countries in the center of this area are usually included as part of the Middle East. However, there are often arguments about countries on the edges of the region. For example should Libya be included instead with other North African states, such as Tunisia, Algeria, and Morocco? Is Afghanistan too Asian to be included? Is the Sudan too African? Is the island of Cyprus too European? Many of the inhabitants of Cyprus are Turkish, and there are Arab banks and businesses there, but some people regard Cyprus as European because most of the islanders are Greek. There is something to be said on each side in all cases. However, the Middle East chosen for this book includes the countries of Bahrain, Cyprus, Egypt, Iran, Iraq, Israel, Jordan, Kuwait, Lebanon, Oman, Qatar, Saudi Arabia,

Syria, Turkey, the United Arab Emirates, and the two Yemen Republics.

Inside state boundaries

Just as there are many differences between the countries in the Middle East, there is variety found inside each of them, and not only in the scenery. Within the state boundaries there is often a wide range of peoples with differing languages, religions, customs, and political views. It is only possible to grow food in about five percent of the area of the Middle East, because of the climate. So all these varied peoples have tended to live crowded together in places where water supplies are reliable. While some good things come out of this, it has also created stresses between rival groups. The history of these conflicts can be traced from prehistoric times right up to the present-day crisis caused by the invasion of Kuwait by Iraq.

In January 1991 the United Nations authorized a force to counter the invasion of Kuwait. A total of 29 nations made up of, among others, the United States, Britain, France, Italy, Australia, Canada, Argentina, Kuwait, Morocco, Egypt, Syria, and all the nations of the Arabian Peninsula, with the exception of the two Yemen republics, contributed to this military coalition.

2

The Land and Its Climate

In many of the drier parts of the Middle East, mud is still one of the traditional building materials. Here, in Syria, a whole family works to add a new layer of straw insulation and cover it with buckets of mud. This roof is already over three feet thick. This gives good protection from both heat and cold, but in an earthquake, the whole family could be crushed by the heavy roof.

When the Middle East is described as a region "where continents meet" this is literally correct. During the hundreds of millions of years of the history of the Earth, the huge plates of rock that make up the continents have been drifting very slowly and gradually across the surface of the globe. Australia, Antarctica, and South America were once joined together as one landmass, and long ago North America and Europe were in contact.

The central parts of the ancient continents are now often vast areas of worn-down hard rocks,

which give boring flat scenery. Much of the Sahara is like this, and so are large areas of the Arabian Peninsula, as well as much of the interiors of Iran and Turkey. However, the continental plates are still on the move and, in parts of the Middle East, they are grinding into one another. This frequently causes earthquakes. Many of these are small, but sometimes hundreds of people are killed. Nevertheless, some of the more gradual earth movements have been helpful to humans. Over millions of years, the edges of some plates have bent downward. As this happened, basins were formed that filled up with mud, burying swamp vegetation. This slowly turned into oil and natural gas, which are now important to the whole world.

Mountain ranges
In other places where the plates have been grinding together, they have pushed up spectacular mountains. Some are higher than the Alps in Europe or the Rockies in the United States, whose highest peaks are respectively 15,750 and 14,440 feet high (4,800 and 4,400 meters). Mount Damavand in the Elburz Mountains of Iran reaches 18,600 feet (5,670 meters). It has a permanent snowcap, as does Mount Ararat in Turkey at 16,950 feet (5,165 meters). Noah's Ark is said to have run aground on Mount Ararat! Massive ranges over 10,000 feet (3,000 meters) high occur elsewhere too, in areas as separated as Oman, Yemen, and Lebanon.

Apart from the mountain ranges, there are other parts of the Middle East that can become really cold. Some plains in Turkey and Iran are so

15

high above sea level that midwinter temperatures seldom rise above freezing, and spring frosts can sometimes kill crops. One reason for the cold is that the skies are usually clear. A great deal of the Middle East is cut off by mountains from the oceans that give moisture for clouds. With no clouds to keep it in, heat escapes straight out into space at night. Even in deserts where it is extremely hot by day, it can get very cold once the sun has gone down. Until the present century, at Isfahan in Iran, people used to flood ponds at dusk. At dawn the ice, which had formed under the clear night sky, was collected. Elsewhere, high in the mountains, winter snow used to be stored in pits covered with dead leaves and pine branches. In the summer, the ice blocks were carried on donkeys down to the cities sweltering in the plains below.

Animals and birds

The different conditions in the mountains and plains can support many kinds of animals and birds. Ostriches, Asiatic lions, cheetahs, and lynxes, once common, have become rare in this century. However, there are still vultures, jackals, Arabian wolves, some oryxes, and several kinds of gazelles, as well as many kinds of snakes, including the horned viper. One type of monitor lizard grows to over three feet (one meter).

The way that temperatures can fluctuate even during a single day has affected the desert wildlife. Jerboas and hamsters live in burrows that are cozy by night but keep out the daytime heat. As the cool of night comes to the desert, the air gives up its moisture and dew forms on cold

Although considerable efforts are being made to save some of the rare species of wildlife in the Middle East, some animals like these bears, wolves, and foxes are still hunted for their pelts.

stones. Small desert animals can get enough moisture to survive by licking the stones. In ancient times, people found that they could grow trees in deserts by making stone piles that would cause night dew to form and supply moisture for the tree roots.

Camels can go for long periods without drinking any water, provided that there is enough moisture in the vegetation they eat. Then, when they do get the opportunity to drink, they can swallow many gallons very quickly and then gallop away. This was very necessary for their survival in the wild, when desert lions used to lie in wait at the waterholes. The camel's hump does not contain water. It is made of fat, which is a good insulator. This fat protects the camel from the sun by day, and keeps its back warm at night!

Plant life

The dry heat of the desert makes it difficult for soils to develop. Dead vegetation shrivels up and blows away instead of rotting and being washed down into the ground. It takes a lot of water to make up for the evaporation caused by the sun's power. With air temperatures of over 100°F

Although plants like these have developed special kinds of leaves and roots that allow them to survive in the salt-encrusted soil of dried-out lake beds, they are of little use to humans and few animals can eat them either.

(40°C) the ground surface can reach nearly 180°F (80°C), a temperature near the boiling point of water. If any rain does fall, everything soon dries out. Much of the Middle East gets no useful rainfall at all and in some parts there may be none for years on end. People can shelter from the sun and wrap up against cold, but lack of water is much harder to endure. This is the main problem of the climate in most of the Middle East.

In the better-watered areas, the natural vegetation would normally be woodland, with trees such as Mediterranean pines, cedars, tamarisks, and oleanders. However, thousands of years of felling, burning, and hungry goats have left very little woodland. In the drier areas there are seldom more than oasis palm trees, camel-thorn scrub, and a few other wild plants that have adapted to harsh desert conditions. Most plants have narrow, spiky leaves that do not catch the sun, with waxy coatings to stop them from drying out. Their seeds and roots can lie in the ground for years, but then grow and flower immediately if there is a shower. Plants like these are not used by humans, though roving herders, called nomads, use them for camels and goats.

Mountain rain
The different climates of the Middle East have played a large part in people's decisions about where to live. In some areas there is so little water that most of the land has been left to the nomads, or is simply unused. Elsewhere, there is enough rain or river water for farming and large permanent settlements. The mountain chains of the Middle East are important, even to people

who do not live within sight of them. They influence the winds, the rainfall, and the temperatures. The winds that bring the most rain come from the west, along the Mediterranean Sea. However, the mountain ranges lining the coasts of Turkey, Lebanon, and Israel wall off much of the interior of the Middle East from the sea. The mountains force the moist air to rise to levels where it is cooler. Cold air is able to hold less water vapor than warm air, so raindrops form. This means that the coastal mountain regions can have as much as 30 to 40 inches of rain each year. The mountains create what is called "rain-shadow" by removing this water from the air, and on the mountains' inland side the land quickly becomes desert.

The "Rain-shadow" Effect

On the inland side of the coastal ranges, the "rain-shadow" effect is very noticeable. Although Damascus is built on the slopes of a range that has high rainfall on its Mediterranean side, the city has a desert climate throughout the summer months. It averages only 9 inches (230 millimeters) of rain a year–less than a quarter of what falls on the mountains nearby.

Cairo, inland in the lowlands of Egypt, averages under one inch (22 millimeters) of rain each year, and in some years virtually none has been recorded (0.06 inch or 1.5 millimeters). Where the rainfall is usually high, people can depend on getting the rain they need each year. In the drier areas, things are often far more difficult because the amount of rain varies greatly from year to year.

This dam was built to irrigate the Chahar Bagh *(the Four Gardens) in Isfahan, Iran, by controlling the waters of the Zeyandeh River. Despite the importance of this river in Isfahan, the desert sun soon completely evaporates its waters and the river never reaches all the way to the sea.*

Many of the streams of the Middle East depend on these mountain rains, and indeed may flow only after a shower. Some watercourses run straight from the hills into the sea. Others go in the opposite direction and drain out of the inland side of the mountains. Many rivers never reach the sea at all. Damascus, the capital of Syria, is called "the gift of the Barada River," since without the river the city could not have developed. Yet this important river soon vanishes when it enters the desert. The same happens to the Zeyandeh River in Iran after it feeds the city of Isfahan. Around half of the Middle East is desert, and people who live there depend on the few rivers mighty enough to resist the evaporating powers of the sun. Even today, the nature of the land has a strong influence on where people settle.

3

Empty Lands—and No Water

People can live almost anywhere on the Earth with enough money and effort. There is even a research base at the South Pole. However, it makes sense to stay where there is drinking water at hand, and land suitable for growing crops. In the Middle East people have been doing this for thousands of years, but recently different choices have become possible with the money that oil has brought. Also, many of the places where oil is found lie out in the desert where nobody had ever settled before, but oil workers must stay there. New methods of making deep wells, learned

People have been watering their flocks like this since ancient times. To take advantage of the night's coolness, the family sleeps outdoors on the brushwood-covered platform in the background.

from the oil industry, have also been used to bring water to the surface. So now crops can be grown and livestock kept in some unlikely places.

Developments such as these have brought great change to some localities, especially in Saudi Arabia, Kuwait, and other Gulf states. However, it does not take many people to run an oil well or modern, mechanized irrigation, so the number of people involved is quite small. Often, the oil money has emphasized old patterns of living, rather than creating completely new ones. Instead of a new network of cities springing up, most of the cities dating back to ancient times have grown larger. Other areas, where there were never many people, have grown even emptier.

Empty wastelands

From prehistoric times right up to the present day, some parts of the Middle East have been virtually empty of people. *Ar Rub' al Khali*, the "Empty Quarter" of the Arabian Peninsula, is one such place, where the sun beats down mercilessly on hundreds of square miles of sand dunes. The *Dasht e Kavir*, the great salt desert of Iran, is another, where only wildlife that has evolved in special ways can survive. Strange gazelles with enormous ears that serve as cooling surfaces, and kidneys adapted to tiny amounts of salty water can be found there. To humans areas like these have always been unproductive wastelands and fearsome wildernesses to cross.

Although most parts of the Middle East are not so extreme in their climate, in many areas a thundershower may wet the ground only once in a quarter of a century. Nomadic herders have found ways of using these places, but usually no fixed settlement is possible. The number of nomads has been getting smaller, particularly since jobs in the oil-rich states offer them easier ways of making a living; so these large areas of the Middle East have become even emptier. Saudi Arabia is the region's largest state and as recently as 1960 half the population were nomads, but now the number is under one in ten. Over the Middle East as a whole, the number is now probably little more than one in 100.

Irrigation

In places where the rainfall is low and unreliable, farming can only be practiced when water is available to water crops artificially, instead of waiting for rain to fall. This is called irrigation.

Sunflowers and melon vines growing in the Fertile Crescent in northern Syria, where enough winter rain falls to support agriculture with relatively little irrigation. In the background, the modern village lies alongside a tell mound, which shows that people have been farming successfully here since prehistoric times, though the desert is not far away.

Irrigation
The importance of irrigation varies from country to country according to the climate. For example, in Kuwait and Egypt, cultivation is simply not possible without irrigation. In terms of the actual sizes of the irrigated areas, some of the countries like Iran and Turkey, which also have rain-fed agriculture, have some of the largest areas of irrigation.

	Irrigated land thousands of acres (hectares)	Percentage of cultivated area
Iran	9,880 (4,000)	30
Egypt	6,100 (2,470)	100
Turkey	5,240 (2,120)	8
Iraq	4,320 (1,750)	32
Syria	1,430 (580)	10
Saudi Arabia	1,000 (405)	36
Israel	540 (220)	50
Lebanon	210 (86)	30
Jordan	90 (38)	9
Kuwait	5 (2)	100

Places in the desert where there are reliable wells or natural springs are called oases. There, in the midst of emptiness, communities can be found growing date palms and cultivating irrigated plots. Some oases support populations of 500 to 1,000 people per sq. mi. (200 to 400 per sq. km.).

Agriculture using rainfall is only possible in a few areas of the Middle East. In the south, in Yemen, Oman, and along the coast of Iran, rain comes in from the Indian Ocean on the great seasonal wind-system called the "monsoon." In the north, the weather from the Mediterranean sweeps across the face of the Turkish mountains and waters the Fertile Crescent of the northern plains of Syria. Although some of the high plains in Turkey and Iran get useful amounts of rain, this comes in winter along with crop-killing frosts. The same problem exists in the water-abundant coastal mountains, whose steep slopes also make farming difficult. Farming in these rain-fed areas can seldom support many people. These days, people are leaving the countryside for the towns. In the steep mountains, where farming has to be done on narrow terraces built along the slopes, depopulation is particularly noticeable. With men leaving for easier jobs in the oil-rich countries, terraces are falling into disrepair.

The biggest farming populations in the Middle East are usually based on irrigation rather than on direct rainfall. An oasis can occur wherever a bed of rock has collected water in such a way that people can get to it. Sometimes the water has been underground for a long time. Some oases in the Sahara and Arabia are pumping up water that sank into the ground thousands of years ago when the climate was wetter. Unfortunately, like the oil, this underground water will soon be depleted in some areas.

Water from the sea
There is, of course, plenty of water in the sea, but it is salty. Desalination is the name used for the process of getting rid of the salt.

Even in parts of the Middle East far from the coast, the groundwater is often salty. There are programs in several countries in which the best water is reserved for humans to drink. Animals and crops that do not like salt come next, then the

Although mountains help produce reliable rainfall, their steep slopes are difficult to farm and it takes a great deal of work to build terraces and keep them in good repair. In many places terraces are now falling apart as people leave for the better jobs in the oil-rich countries.

more resistant crops get the saltier water, and so on. Where necessary, good water is added to some from the less desirable sources to make it usable. In Israel, water is distributed from a national pipeline network. This brings water southward from the rainier north by pipes nearly ten feet (three meters) in diameter.

27

Distributing water

Although pipelines are modern technology, canals have been used for distributing water in the Middle East since prehistoric times. Unlike closed pipes, they lose water by evaporation under the hot sun. However, for at least 2,000 years, underground tunnel-canals called *qanats* have been used to get around this problem. Some run for miles, but often the only hint of their existence is a line of marks like bomb craters on the surface. These marks show where the diggers used vertical shafts to remove the earth from the tunnel beneath. Though *qanats* were once widespread (the Arabs even built some in Spain), most of those still in use are in Iran.

Even with today's technology, the amount of water moved by human efforts is tiny compared with that brought into dry areas of the Middle East by the few great rivers. Despite the importance of oil nowadays, the water brought by these rivers is still as vital a factor in where people live as it was in ancient times.

4   Great Rivers, Long Distances

Along the great rivers, crops are grown on the rich bottomlands made of silt brought down by the river, but the villages are often placed on the rocky slopes above. There they are clear of floods and do not use up the precious farming land. On the slopes they are also sheltered from the scorching winds that blow across the barren desert above the cliffs. This village is on the Euphrates.

There are three rivers of special importance to the people of the Middle East. From the north come the Tigris and Euphrates, and from the south, the Nile. The first two rise in the highlands of Turkey. The Euphrates loops through Syria before joining the Tigris in Iraq to flow into the head of the Gulf of Arabia. Mesopotamia is the name for the land between them. *"Potamoi"* is ancient Greek for river and "Meso-potamia" simply means "between the rivers." Although little rain ever falls there, irrigation allowed Mesopotamia to become one of the ancient world's great centers of

civilization, with cities like Babylon and Nineveh. Then, in medieval times while Paris and London were still tiny, Baghdad, now in Iraq, was a sophisticated Islamic city many times their size. Although the annual floods of these three rivers can bring wealth by irrigating the desert, they can also bring disaster. The Tigris can rise at a rate of one foot (30 centimeters) an hour, and floods of 33 feet (10 meters) are not unknown.

Egypt and the Nile

The Nile is the longest river in the world (4,160 miles, 6,695 kilometers). The main branch, the White Nile, is fed by the torrential rains of central Africa. Water from the Ethiopian highlands in East Africa is added where the Blue Nile joins the White at Khartoum in the Sudan. The Pharaohs spoke of the Red and Black Land of Egypt, and this is still true today. The Red Land is the almost uninhabitable desert. The Black is the well-watered, rich, muddy strip of soil provided by the Nile. Including the delta below Cairo, the Black Land only covers three percent of Egypt's area, yet 90 percent of the population of around 50 million people live on it. There are more than 1,300 people per sq. mi. (500 per sq. km.) on most of the Black Land, and as many as 5,200 per sq. mi. (2,000 per sq. km.) in parts of the delta. This is remarkable for land with almost no rainfall, and shows how important rivers are to the people of the Middle East.

Cairo, the capital of Egypt, is now the second biggest city in the world, with over 14 million people living in the built-up areas on both sides of the Nile.

Most freight is now carried by heavy trucks, and camel caravans of the kind that carried goods through the Middle East for thousands of years are rare. However, sometimes they can still be seen. In Turkey, it is traditional for the line of camels to be led by a donkey.

Road and rail transportation

In eastern North America and Europe, towns tend to merge into one another, but in the Middle East empty deserts often separate settlements. Since ancient times, goods have been carried on pack camels, using trails stretching as far as China. Chains of *caravanserai* developed. These were bandit-proof stopping places at waterholes a day's march apart. The distances are so great, and there are so few people, that many areas even now only have small dirt roads. However, most nations have a basic network of all-weather roads, often built for military reasons. Today, overland freight comes mainly by heavy trucks, from as far as Europe and India. Railroads are less important than roads, though some

31

As the Middle East has developed, good roads have been built through the desert and mountains to carry the increasing amount of traffic moving between the cities.

modernization is going on. Some urban railway systems are being developed. Long-distance buses are popular for travel between cities. Thousands of pilgrims go by bus to Mecca each year, and crowded buses come all the way from Afghanistan and Istanbul.

Water transportation
Despite the dry climate, water transportation has always been important. People used to float rafts down the Tigris River, then the rafts' timber was sold profitably along with their cargoes in treeless Mesopotamia. For centuries *dhows*, the local wooden trading vessels, used the seasonal winds to sail all the way to southern Africa to pick up mangrove poles for house building in the

timberless Gulf states. Although little wooden skiffs of this kind are still built, they all have engines now. Times have changed quickly, and today Bahrain has a worldwide reputation for high technology ship repair work. Nowadays, the Gulf is busy with supertankers from Iran and the Arab oil producers.

One crucial step in the development of water transportation in the Middle East was the cutting of the Suez Canal, completed in 1869. This 114 mile (184 kilometer) waterway linked the Mediterranean to the Red Sea, and thus the Atlantic to the Indian Ocean. By making it unnecessary to sail around Africa, it took weeks off voyages between the Middle East and many other parts of the world, cutting some distances by over 40 percent. However, the canal is much less important than it used to be.

The immense size of modern oil tankers means that once again many have to sail around Africa instead of using the Suez Canal, which was designed for the much smaller sailing ships and steamers of the nineteenth century.

Air transportation

Many supertankers and bulk carriers are now too large to go through the canal, and aircraft have taken over most passenger traffic from ocean liners.

Partly because of the importance of the oil business, the Middle East is well provided with satellite communications and air routes. However, the airlines do not only serve the oil company executives and employees. Mecca is one of the most important pilgrimage destinations in the region. Of the million or so Muslims who go there each year, not all travel by bus or pilgrim ship. Many fly in from Islamic communities as far away as the United States, Britain, Nigeria, Pakistan, and Indonesia.

5 Many Languages, Many Religions

Although most people in the Middle East speak Arabic, this is not true of all of them. However, it is a major advantage that over such a large area most people can speak to one another directly, in the same way that similar numbers of North Americans share English. Europe, on the other hand, may have its Economic Community, but it lacks a common language.

The three countries in the Middle East with the largest populations are Iran, Turkey, and Egypt, each with around 50 million people. Most Egyptians are Arabic speakers, but the main languages of the other two, Turkish and Iran's Persian (Farsi), are quite different. These differences can be shown simply by counting up to five in each language:

	ONE	TWO	THREE	FOUR	FIVE
Arabic:	*Wahid*	*Itnen*	*Tlatey*	*Arba*	*Hamsa*
Turkish:	*Bir*	*Iki*	*Ooch*	*Dort*	*Besh*
Farsi:	*Yek*	*Do*	*Seh*	*Chahar*	*Panj*

The words above have been spelled using the western alphabet. This is to give some idea of the sound of each word to people who are used to reading English. However, the Middle Eastern languages have their own forms of lettering. Even the Turks, who have adopted a version of the western alphabet, use it slightly differently from the way it is used here.

Arabic

Arabic is very different from European languages. The Arabs write from right to left, and their words often change their vowel sounds like "sIng, sAng, sUng, sOng" in English. Arabic uses sounds that no single European letter can describe. For this reason, and because of all the vowel changes, Arabic words may be spelled in many different ways in the European alphabet. Thus the name of the Prophet of Islam may be found written as Mahommet, Mohammed, Muhammed, or Mehmet. The Holy Book may be spelled Koran, or Quran, and Mecca as Makkah. Sheikh is the commonest English version of the Arabic title for the head of a noble family, tribe, or clan, and it is also a polite way of addressing scholars or dignitaries. It is sometimes written as Sheik, Shaikh, or even Xeq. There are similar problems in representing the other Middle Eastern languages in western lettering.

Samples of Different Kinds of Writing Used in the Middle East

في البدي كان الكلمة — Arabic

Ակզբումն էր Բանն — Armenian

בראשית היה הדבר — Hebrew

'Εν ἀρχῇ ἦν ὁ λόγος. — Greek

These examples are all translations of "In the beginning was the Word," from the Bible (John: Chapter I, Verse 1)

Hebrew

Despite the differences between Israelis and Arabs, their languages are much closer than are Turkish and Arabic. After the state of Israel was set up in 1948, the Jews who moved there from all over the world spoke many languages. The Israeli government has used a re-creation of the ancient Hebrew language as a way of strengthening their feeling of unity. Hebrew and Arabic come from the same roots.

Persian and Kurdish

In Iran several languages are spoken, but the main one is Persian (Farsi). This is of the Indo-European family of languages and is closer grammatically to some languages of the Indian subcontinent and Europe than it is to Arabic.

These Kurdish men are in Amuda in northeast Syria.

Turkish is quite different from either, having come from central Asia. Another Indo-European language is Kurdish. There are well over ten million Kurds, but they do not have a state of their own and live in parts of Turkey, Iran, Syria, and Iraq. Their use of their own language strengthens their feeling that they are a distinctive people. The same is true of the Armenian-speakers who are spread throughout the Middle East and part of the Soviet Union. They also have their own form of lettering.

Most Armenians are Christian. There are many groups of Christians in the Middle East, but the largest number is to be found in Egypt, where about one in ten of the population is Christian. The majority of these Christians belong to the Coptic Church, whose service books are written in the Coptic language. The Coptic language has developed from the ancient Egyptian language.

Three great religions
Judaism, Christianity, and Islam all started in the Middle East, and spread to other parts of the world from there. There are now about 200 million Muslims in the Middle East, and more than 600 million elsewhere, mostly in Pakistan, Bangladesh, and Indonesia. There are about 40 million in the Soviet Union.

Through the centuries, other people's ideas, as varied as Greek philosophy from Europe and Hinduism from India, have entered the Middle East, influencing existing religions and also helping to inspire new faiths. For example, Bahaism developed in Iraq and has now spread around the world. There have also been disagreements within each of the main religions. From all this, a whole range of different groups has emerged, each with its own set of beliefs. Some, such as the Druze and Yazidis, are unique to the region.

Even the four million Israeli Jews, a fairly small number, are divided into different groups. They are mainly Sephardim from North Africa and the Middle East, and Ashkenazim from America and Europe. There are literally dozens of Christian groups. The most numerous after the Copts of Egypt, who number six million, are the one million Maronites in Lebanon.

Despite this remarkable variety of religions, more than nine people out of ten in the Middle East are Muslims. They too are divided into groups, such as the Alawi, Wahabi, Ibadi, and

In Egypt, the outsides of many mosques are left as bare stone, but the masonry is carved in patterns that show up beautifully in the strong sunlight. This example is in Cairo.

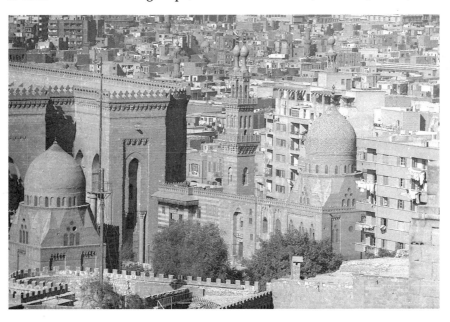

many others. By far the largest group are the Sunnis, dominating the Arabian Peninsula, Turkey, and North Africa. However, there are some 50 million Shi'ite Muslims forming majorities in Iraq and Iran and important minorities in Lebanon, Syria, Yemen AR, and Oman.

Despite all this diversity, the three great religions of the Middle East share common roots. For example, *Id el Adha*, the Feast of the Sacrifice, is the greatest feast of the Muslim year. It marks the faith of Abraham, which was so great that he was ready to obey God's request to sacrifice his only son, Isaac. God relented and allowed him to substitute a ram. Now, Muslim families who can afford it have a sheep slaughtered in the ritual way, and give the meat to the poor. Since the saving of a young boy is being celebrated, it is a great day for children.

Jerusalem

Although this feast is so much part of the Muslim year, Jews regard Abraham as one of the great fathers of their religion. Their king Solomon built a great temple at Jerusalem, where their holy book of the law, the *Torah*, gained its final form. The Arabs conquered Palestine in the early seventh century A.D. Soon afterward they built the Dome of the Rock where Solomon's Temple had stood. This was to emphasize that Islam was to replace Judaism and Christianity. In the Muslim tradition, the rock bears the hoof print of Muhammad's winged horse, Buraq.

Jerusalem is also central to the Christian faith. Jesus grew up in a Jewish community, and there is continuity with this heritage in his teaching. However, followers who believed he had risen from the dead gradually broke away from the mainstream of Jewish religion. Christians regard Jesus as the Son of God. This is very different from Muslim belief. Muhammad certainly did not have that view of himself, nor of any other prophet. He called himself a "Messenger of God." There have been as many as 40,000 "Messengers" recognized by Islam. These include Abraham and Jesus, but none of them, including Muhammad,

In Iran, mosques are often made from mud bricks covered with brightly colored ceramic tiles displaying sayings from the Koran. This one is in Isfahan.

41

was considered divine, as Jesus is by Christians. Muslims believe that God's revelation to Muhammad is the complete and final one.

Islamic beliefs

Muslims believe that the Message came to Muhammad in a very direct way. The Angel Gabriel commanded him to recite. The word *Koran* means "recitation," and the book records what the faithful believe are the actual words of God as revealed through his Prophet Muhammad. These were written down during his lifetime on anything handy, from papyrus to the shoulder-blade bones of camels, then collected as the sacred *Koran*. The word Islam

---

The Five Pillars of Islam

1 There is no God but God, and Muhammad is the Prophet of God. This is part of what the *muezzin* traditionally calls from the minaret of a mosque to bring the faithful to prayer.

2 Muslims pray five times daily. The worshiper should be in a state of purity, which is symbolized by ritual washing in a ritually clean place, and facing Mecca where the Prophet was born.

3 A fast is kept during the whole month of Ramadan, taking neither food nor drink from sunrise until sunset. Since the Islamic calendar reckons months by the moon, the date of Ramadan shifts each year. When it falls in the full heat of the summer, it takes great devotion to drink nothing until sunset.

4 Muslims should give alms to the poor.

5 They should try to make the pilgrimage, known as the *Hajj*, to Mecca at least once in their lifetime.

---

means "submission to God," and Muslim means "one who submits."

The five principles or Five Pillars of Islam are shared by all the many Muslim groups. However, Muslims often differ passionately over other aspects of their beliefs, as well as seeing things differently from those who follow other faiths.

This rich variety of religions has enriched the cultural and artistic life of the Middle East and of the world. Unfortunately both in the past and at the present day, the sincerity and strength with which these different beliefs are held has also led to bitter conflicts and persecutions. These form a theme that runs through the history of the area.

6   Living with History

In the Middle East, history is very much a part of present-day life. In the first place, it is necessary to know the history of the groups people belong to, in order to understand why different groups react to one another in certain ways. Secondly, since people have tended to live in the same places with reliable water supplies, century after century, there are reminders of history even in today's busy cities. For example, in the center of a town like Aleppo in Syria there is a great mound of rubble. This rubble is from mud-brick buildings, and the mound started to build up in prehistoric times when the whole idea of towns was new. On top of the mound is a castle built to

The Citadel of Aleppo is a castle built to resist the Crusaders. It is set on a great tell.

In the Middle East it is not only large towns like Aleppo that have reused the same sites since ancient times. There are many small settlements like this one near the Turkish-Syrian border, where the modern village is beside or on top of a tell mound strewn with prehistoric pottery.

resist Crusaders. This is still used by the present government. Nearby, the modern market still shows the rectangular street grid laid out by Roman planners. Other parts of the town are also on a grid, but this was set out by the French in the colonial period of this century.

Two empires

Although the same sites have been built on, time after time, the history they reveal is one of constant change, with different groups dominating the area in turn. At the time of Christ, large parts of the Middle East were in the Roman Empire. When the western part of the Empire, centered on Rome itself, collapsed in the fifth century A.D., the Eastern or Byzantine Empire managed to survive. It ruled Asia Minor, now

Turkey, Syria, and Egypt, as a Christian empire.

Meanwhile, another great empire had been developing in western Asia, created by the Sassanids of Persia. They blocked the trade of Byzantium to the east. The Byzantines fought back, and the two empires went on struggling, gradually becoming exhausted. They were quite unable to cope with the event that changed the whole course of history in the Middle East. This was the coming of Islam, and a wave of Arab conquests that carried the new religion far beyond its Arabian homeland.

Muhammad's ideas took root in the early seventh century, and within 80 years the Arabs had conquered an area larger than the Romans had acquired in eight centuries. To the west, they took over North Africa and Spain and even struck into France, where they were stopped at the battle of Poitiers in A.D.732. To the east, they kept going until, in A.D.751, they met a Chinese army at the battle of Talas, east of Samarkand.

The Crusades

The Arabs did not have it all their own way. In 1096 the Crusades started, and for two centuries there were European invasions of the Middle East. Several small states were set up by the Europeans in the area that is now Israel, Lebanon, western Syria, and southern Turkey guarded by spectacular castles like Krak des Chevaliers.

The Crusaders had some inspiring leaders, such as Richard Lion-hearted, King of England. However, in the end they were outmatched by Middle Easterners like the Kurdish leader Salah

Krak des Chevaliers, or the Carrack (great ship) of the Knights. This castle was built by Crusaders, the Knights of St. John, in what is now the borderland between Syria and north Lebanon. It was so strong even Saladin failed to capture it.

ud Din, called Saladin by the Europeans. In 1187 he retook Jerusalem for Islam, and eventually Krak and all the other Christian strongholds had to be abandoned. When the last one, Acre, fell in 1291, the Crusades in the Middle East were over.

While the Crusades had been going on, waves of Turkish nomads had been coming west from Central Asia. In the eleventh century, Seljuk Turks took Baghdad and went on into Asia Minor. Ottoman Turks seized Constantinople, capital of the Byzantine Empire, in 1453, renaming it Istanbul. By the seventeenth century, the Turkish Sultans ruled much of Eastern Europe and North Africa, as well as the Middle East. As late as 1683, they were in Austria, using armored camels to attack Vienna.

47

The Ottoman Empire gradually disintegrated during the nineteenth century and was eventually replaced by the Turkish Republic in 1923. In the meantime, European colonial powers such as France and Britain took over parts of the Middle East. Egypt came under British rule in 1882. After World War I, France took over the government of Lebanon and Syria, while the British ran southern Iraq.

Civil wars within states

The colonial era is over, but independence did not bring peace. Every country in the Middle East has suffered from internal conflicts in recent decades, apart from the tiny states of Qatar, Bahrain, and the Emirates.

Part of the problem has been the lack, in many states, of effective ways of sharing decisions when there are disagreements. In the histories of the United States, the United Kingdom, and Australia, democracy has had several hundred years to develop. These democratic systems are by no means perfect, but they work reasonably well, offering a way of changing a government peacefully. However, history has not made it easy for the Middle Eastern countries to develop systems of government to suit their particular needs. Some areas have been under the rule of a single person right into the twentieth century. For example, the Sultan was at the head of the Ottoman Empire, and the Shah ruled Iran until 1979. Military strongmen have also taken control, sometimes offering a deliberate break from the past, such as the reshaping of Egypt by Colonel Gamal Abdul Nasser.

Calendars
One complication of living in the Middle East is that several different calendars are used. Businessmen have to allow for the holy day of each week falling on Friday for Muslims, Saturday for Jews, and Sunday for Christians.

Muslims count their years from the time of the *Hijra*, when the Prophet had to flee from Mecca to Medina to found his new religion. That was in A.D. 622 of the Christian calendar.

The Muslim year is based on months measured by the appearance of the new moon, and 12 such months only add up to 354 days. By following these months the religious festivals, such as Ramadan, fall 11 days earlier each year. Instead of using leap years, an extra day is put in 11 times in every 30 years. Fortunately, the two calendars sometimes match in round numbers. Thus, year 1400 *Hijra* on the Muslim calendar was 1980 in Western terms.

To save confusion in international dealings, in most Arab countries, the Western calendar is used for official and business purposes, although the Muslim months are used for religious events. The Western months are given these names:

January	=	*Kanoon al Thani*
February	=	*Shabat*
March	=	*Adhar*
April	=	*Nisan*
May	=	*Mayiss* or *Ayar*
June	=	*Haziran*
July	=	*Tamus*
August	=	*Ab*
September	=	*Ayul*
November	=	*Tshrine al Awwal*
December	=	*Kanoon al Awwal*

Religion as a factor

Religion has also been a very important force in modern Middle Eastern politics, powerful both in bonding people together and in dividing them. The replacement of the Shah in Iran by the regime of the Ayatollah Ruhollah Khomeini was a notable example of this. Religion is also a major factor in the troubles in Lebanon, and between the Palestinians and Israelis.

Border wars

History has left problems between the states, as well as inside them. Many of their international borders follow straight lines drawn up in political deals made in the colonial period. These often cut across physical features, and ignore the complicated patterns of languages and religious groupings as well as the feelings of minorities. The Kurds, for example, are split between four countries. Since 1945 there have been 20 border wars between the states of the Middle East. Thus, although the two main war zones of recent years have been the Israel/Syria/Lebanon area and the Iraq/Iran frontier, few other parts of the Middle East have avoided bloodshed. Many of the historical reasons for conflict in the Middle East still exist, and may well lead to more trouble in the future. Most recently the disagreement between Kuwait and Iraq over the extent of the oil field the two nations share sparked the Iraqi invasion of Kuwait in 1990.

7   How Nomads Live

Films about the Middle East often show Bedouin nomads riding camels from oasis to oasis, far out in the desert. The number of Middle Easterners who used to live that kind of roving life was never large, compared to village farmers or city dwellers. Today the number of true nomads, who spend much of their lives on the move, is very small indeed. Now they use diesel trucks and herd sheep and goats, so camels are quite difficult to find. As with horses in America, Europe, or Australia, camels are now often kept for sporting purposes. For thousands of years, nomadism was the only way that most of the land in the Middle East could be used, because crops could only be grown where the supply of water was reliable.

Nomads and conservation
Nomads learned by experience just how to cope with their difficult environment. They often owned the oases, and farmers there worked for them. Instead of waiting for water to come to them, nomads took their animals to graze wherever rain had happened to fall in any particular year. The lifestyle they created conserved the fragile environment for future generations of the tribe. There are now so few nomads left that vast areas where their flocks once grazed are no longer used in any way at all. Such places are more empty now than they have been for many centuries.

There are several reasons for the decline in the

Much of the grazing land of the Middle East is rocky, and with such sparse vegetation it is easy to see why flocks have to keep on the move if they are to find enough to eat.

number of nomads. Many young men have given up herding to work on building sites in places like Kuwait and Saudi Arabia, where the wages are good. Also, few governments like independent-minded nomads who ride away into neighboring states whenever they are asked to pay taxes or do military service. The nomads have either been forced to live in one place or have been given incentives to stay. Some have been offered wells that supply water throughout the year. Although this may help to solve political problems, it can create environmental ones instead. Herders who are real nomads keep moving on to fresh pastures, and the areas they leave can recover. However, when settled permanently at a well, their herds eat up everything within a day's walk of the water supply. Once this plant cover is destroyed the wind soon creates a dust bowl, making the area useless for future generations.

Kurds and Bedouin

Now that long-distance camel herding is vanishing, many nomads take only short journeys, not over desert plains but into the mountains. Conditions there are unpleasant in winter, so herders, such as the Kurds, spend winter with their flocks at permanent villages at the foot of the mountains. When spring comes and the snows melt, they take their animals, which are usually sheep and goats, with some cattle, up the mountains to get the benefit of the lush high pastures in the summer.

In some areas, for example between the mountains of Turkey and plains of Syria, there

A village in Azerbaijan in Iran, crouched at the mounain foot where the desert begins. This is the kind of settlement that is the base for people who shelter in the lowlands and then take their flocks up to the pastures high above when the harsh winter is over.

used to be a double movement of people of different cultures who depended on different animals. During the winter, while the Kurds were at the mountain foot, the Bedouin would be far out on the plains, taking advantage of the winter season of rain to find grazing for their camels. Then, as summer came on and the Kurds moved their flocks up to the high pastures, the desert became too hot for comfort and the vegetation there withered. The Bedouin then came back to the springs at the mountain foot where the Kurdish villages were. There the two communities traded goods and the products of their different animals. The sensible Bedouin thus kept out of the desert during the hottest part of the year. This was the time when they rested with their animals at reliable waterholes. Then, as soon as it became cool enough, they would set off once more. They would leave as much as possible of the grazing around the waterholes, so that it would see them through the next summer.

The Bedouin of Damascus
The distances nomads traveled varied from year to year. When the rains were good, there was plenty of grazing and the waterholes were full, so they did not need to go far. In bad years they had to use all the tribe's knowledge to search out every scrap of grazing and every drop of water. Sometimes this meant hundreds of miles of trekking. For example, Bedouin families based near Damascus would spend the hot season resting near the city, where they could trade their goods and animal produce. There, at the edge of the rain-catching mountains, there were wells

they could rely on and they had vegetables and fruit from irrigated gardens. When winter came, they would head out on a great sweeping loop through the desert. The drier the year, the farther they had to go. The main party of each family, with the old people and baggage, would follow the simplest route. Each day the children would move out at an angle from that path, taking their sheep and goats to whatever grazing was nearby. If there was not enough, men would go off on the faster camels. Sometimes they would be away for days on end, searching for grazing and water. One of the most reliable places was a long valley, the Wadi es Sirhan. Instead of going directly there at the start of the season, all the tribes accepted that it should be left until last. No matter what blood feuds or camel raids were going on between them, they agreed to preserve the valley as a safe route homeward to Damascus when the rest of the grazing was gone.

Nomad homes
For families always on the move, tent homes are a vital part of their equipment. The long, low, dark tents of the Bedouin, though they seem simple, are the product of thousands of years of learning to deal with the harsh desert environment. They are made from goat hair, woven by the women on portable looms. In dry conditions the haircloth lets air through, but if there is a downpour the weave closes up and becomes waterproof. The tents are black, and since black absorbs heat, the cloth gets hot, but gives a deep, restful shade. With the side curtains up, the tents make the most of any cooling breeze, but their low shape is also

Camped Bedouin wait for the herders to bring their sheep, camels, and goats back from the daily search for grazing. Although they are far from any permanent settlement and belong to the same group, note how the families have, for privacy, pitched their tents apart rather than side by side.

good for resisting the gusts of a sandstorm.

Unlike black, white and other light colors reflect the heat, so light-colored clothing and headdresses are usually worn in the Middle East. However, the glare of a white surface can be hard on the eyes, so desert travelers often wear a dark upper cloak.

A tradition of hospitality

Usually several families travel together. Even when they know one another well, nomadic families like to be private. They use the space of the desert to secure this, by pitching their tents far apart. This does not mean that the nomadic peoples of the Middle East are unsociable. On the contrary, they have a strong tradition of hospitality. In the past, if a stranger was turned away into the desert without food and water, it could mean his death. His hosts could be the next travelers needing help. Even now, in sophisticated city society in the Middle East, it is still thought to be bad manners to allow visitors to leave without offering them coffee or tea.

8   Farming and Food

Few people now live as nomads, but another traditional lifestyle, that of the farmer, is still important in the Middle East. Even in the present oil age, farming still employs more people than any other activity. Despite the enormous growth of cities, many Middle Easterners are still country people, living in villages. While nomads can move their flocks as they need to, farmers need a dependable supply of water to grow crops. Rainfall is reliable enough for farming mainly near coastal mountains and on northern plains, and there villages can spread out across the landscape. Elsewhere farming is often only possible by irrigating the land with additional

From the air, Lake Nasser looks like an inland sea. However, in its creation, the fertile lands along the old course of the Nile have been submerged and lost. As the photograph shows, nothing grows where the water of the reservoir meets the red sands of the desert.

water. So where there are oases with reliable springs or wells, people crowd together. Where there is a dependable river, they live in a row of villages strung like beads along it. Both in Mesopotamia and along the Nile, big irrigation systems were developed over 5,000 years ago.

Water technology

These days dams are used not only to store water but to create hydroelectric power. This is particularly important to countries that have a fairly small amount of oil but have great rivers, such as Syria and Egypt. There are massive turbine generators for electricity in al Tabqa Dam on the Euphrates and the Aswan High Dam on the Nile. The reservoirs created behind these dams, Lake Assad and Lake Nasser, are so large that they allow "water banking." This means that water from good years can be saved up, and released during drought years.

High technology has affected irrigation in other ways as well. Now there are motorized, mobile spray systems, and networks of plastic pipes to drip-feed individual plants. However, the "technology" developed in ancient times is still effective, and much less expensive. The *shaduf* is a lever with a weight at one end to balance the weight of a bucket of water, making the bucket easier to lift. The *noria* is a great wooden waterwheel, turned by the river itself, with scoops that carry the water up to a high-level aqueduct. Both can still be seen in Syria, at Hama on the Orontes River. Boys cling onto the wheel as if it were a fairground ride, then dive off the top into the river over 50 feet (15 meters) below.

A corner of a farming village on the Syrian-Turkish border. Since there are no grassy fields to graze, the cow is coming in to be fed, like the horse and calf, on a mixture of straw and greens, which are partly from irrigated fodder crops and partly leaves cut from trees. Grain has been spread on the flat roof to dry out. It will be used to make bread and bulgur (parched wheat).

Crops and irrigation

Which crops are grown in different parts of the Middle East depends on how much water is available, and how pure it is. Cotton, the most important of the nonfood crops, usually needs irrigation, although rain does help in parts of the north. It is grown mainly in Egypt, Iran, Syria, and Turkey. Where there is enough rain, the emphasis is usually on grains, particularly wheat and barley. The main corn crop is grown under irrigation in Egypt. Irrigation has been used to grow grain in Mesopotamia since prehistoric days. In ancient times farmers there had to change from wheat to barley, because of a build-up of salts in the soil. Barley tolerates salt better.

Even with modern knowledge, land is still

The result of badly managed irrigation. Too much water has been used on this land and the evaporation by the fierce sun has created a salt crust from the chemicals in the soil, killing the plants.

being ruined in parts of the Middle East because of poor irrigation methods. People often assume that the more water is put on the land, the better. However, the sun is so hot that any extra water not used immediately by the plants is drawn back up to the surface, bringing with it soil salts. These form a hard crust that poisons the plants.

Because irrigation costs money, crops that need a lot of water are usually only grown when they offer a good profit. For example, root crops are seldom important in the Middle East, although Egypt and Cyprus find it profitable to grow early-season potatoes for European supermarkets. However, fresh green vegetables have always been appreciated in these hot lands. Now there is a rising demand for fresh produce for the rapidly growing cities throughout the Middle East, and also for Europe. The commercial production of vegetables has expanded, and Israel and Jordan have both developed export markets. The same is happening with fruit, which now represents half the agricultural production of Cyprus, Lebanon, and Israel. Apples, pears, cherries, and hazelnuts are grown mainly in the northern uplands, in Turkey for example, while most oranges, lemons, and grapefruit come from the Mediterranean coastal lowlands. Dates, the traditional oasis crop, are also exported.

Importing foods

Despite expanded farming, large quantities of food still have to be imported into the Middle East. On the one hand there is the harsh, hot

The parts of the bazaars of the Middle East where they sell fruits and vegetables tend to be lively places, full of color and attractive scents.

climate with its lack of water and scarcity of good land, and on the other hand the very rapid increase of the population. In the late 1980s, food imports sometimes accounted for nearly a third of the region's total revenue from oil.

There has been talk about using the food weapon as a threat against the Middle East if oil prices rise too high. This made the Saudi Arabians determined to show that they could become self-sufficient, at least in wheat. They offered their farmers ten times the world's average price for a ton of wheat grown in Saudi Arabia. By using high-technology methods, with mobile irrigation rigs on many miles of strip plots out in the desert, wheat production was increased from just 3,000 tons a year to well over a million tons a year. Saudi Arabia has thus safeguarded itself and can also offer some food security to other Gulf states.

Eating and drinking

Although getting enough to eat and drink remains a problem in the Middle East, people have always enjoyed coming together for meals or refreshments. Coffee is an important symbol of hospitality, in a city apartment and in a nomad's tent. Coffee drinking started in the Middle East and, although most of the world's supply is now grown in the Americas and East Africa, mocha beans from the Yemen mountains first led to coffee's popularity.

Just as coffee has been popularized around the world, so too have many Middle Eastern foods. Today, *halva*, sesame seeds and honey, or a *kebab* of spit-roasted meat can be bought from

Massachusetts to Melbourne. The kebab is often served with *pitta*, the characteristic flat bread of the Middle East. Bread is eaten with most meals, but a main course can be made from a number of different bases. These may be bulgur (parched wheat), chickpeas, beans, or rice, seasoned with onions, garlic, herbs, and spices. Since ancient times, the Middle East has been the crossroads of the spice routes from Africa and the Far East. One favorite spice mix is cinnamon with nutmeg, cloves, and ginger. Saffron, which is made from the crocus flower, gives a more delicate flavor and dyes food a glorious yellow. Yellow food is believed to bring happiness and laughter.

Chicken dishes are very popular, but pigs are never eaten by Jews or Muslims. For any meat to be acceptable to them, the animals have to be killed according to ritual procedures. Mutton is the most usual meat, and large numbers of sheep are imported, particularly from Australia.

A meal can end with an extraordinary range of pastries, preserves, and honey cakes. There is a tradition in the Middle East that sweet things sweeten life and drive off sadness.

9   Family Life

Besides food, people need clothes. Parts of the Middle East get extremely cold in winter. The Iranians, Turks, and Kurds who live in the mountains and on the high plains now often wear modern-style windproof clothes. However, some of the shepherds still value cloaks made out of the traditional felt. The felt is made without

Different regions still have their own styles of dress. This is everyday wear in part of Syria.

64

The traditional headdress of the Middle East is cool and practical.

weaving, by matting wool together, and the cloaks are so stiff they can almost stand up by themselves.

In some ways, cold is easier to cope with than heat, since more clothes can be added to keep warm. In the glare of the desert, simply taking clothes off does not solve problems. Protection is needed from the sunlight, and from the heat bouncing up from the ground. Tight clothes are soon soaked with sweat and then help the sun to draw vital moisture from the body. The answer is to wear several layers of loose clothing. The air caught in this is the best insulation from the heat outside. It is not just because of pride in their traditional dress that people of the Middle East prefer their robes and headdresses to western-style clothes. Their flowing robes are cooler and far more comfortable.

Buildings that stay cool

After food and clothes, the third thing people need is a structure to provide shelter. Traditional buildings of the Middle East show the benefit of centuries of experience in coping with heat. Thick mud-brick walls and a roof made of layers of straw and mud keep out the summer's heat, and yet give a home that is easily warmed in winter.

In the villages and in older parts of the towns, buildings are usually crowded close together, giving one another shelter. The narrow alleys are shaded by upper storeys that jut out.

Sometimes, complete streets are roofed over, to give a covered market. The one at Isfahan in Iran is covered by a series of elegant domes, each with a small central hole. The wind speeds up to rise over the domes and, as it does so, it sucks out stale air from inside, providing air conditioning without expensive machinery. Nearby, there are houses with wind towers, once much more common in the Middle East. The hollow towers catch any wind and pass it down into the house as a cooling breeze. Even when there is no wind

The bazaar in Isfahan is roofed with a chain of domes, each with a central hole that draws out the stale air from inside the bazaar.

outside, if it is hot inside the house the warm air rises up the tower, starting a cool draft below.

Many of the buildings with wind towers were courtyard houses. This used to be a favorite kind of family home in the Middle East, offering several advantages. At night, heat escaped up into the cloudless skies. Then when dawn came the shady courtyard was like a pool of cold air. Since cool air is heavier than warm, it remained there as the land around began to heat up. Trees and plants in the courtyard, and perhaps a little fountain, helped to keep the place pleasantly

The shady courtyard of a fine house in Syria. Far into the day, the fountain and the greenery help to keep the coolness of the night air trapped in the courtyard.

cool. The courtyard also gave security, which was very important in an area with such a history of conflict. There was usually only one entrance, fitted with heavy doors that could be firmly barred. There were few or no outside windows at street level, which gave a third advantage, privacy. Nomads could use the space of the desert to achieve this, but for dwellers in the tightly packed towns, the inward-looking courtyard house formed a practical solution to the problem.

Muslim women
Whether the housing is old-style or modern, the tradition of privacy in family life remains very strong in most of the Middle East. This is often expressed through the behavior expected of women. When visitors come to a home, it is still usual for men to be entertained in one room, and women in another.

Although in many of the countries of the Middle East some women wear western clothes and work outside the home in offices, or in professions such as medicine or teaching, very many women still follow the traditional Islamic pattern of life. A woman is seldom seen walking alone through the streets, and men may do the family shopping so that their wives do not need to go out alone.

In parts of the Middle East, women cover their faces with a veil in public, and indeed are often covered from head to foot in an all-enveloping *chadur* or *burqa*. The custom of wearing veils has been reinforced recently with the growth of fundamentalist Islam and a return to the original traditions of the Muslim faith. Even where the veil is not worn, women usually cover their heads and hair in public.

Marriage

Most Muslim girls marry while quite young. Marriages are not always arranged, but it is still usual for a girl of any age to ask her parents' approval before she marries. Marriages are regarded as involving two whole families rather than just two individuals. Though divorce is allowed by Islam, these family ties make it a serious matter. Wedding celebrations can be noisy, with overloaded cars roaring through the streets, horns blaring, women singing, and men firing shots into the air. Feasting may go on for as long as three days. In Syria there is a special wedding soup made of sheep's feet and garlic-flavored yogurt.

The Koran permits a man to marry up to four wives, but only if he believes he can be fair to them all equally. However, it is unusual for a man to take several wives. A survey taken in Egypt recently has shown that only one in 25 has more than one wife.

10 Towns and Cities

In the first rush of oil prosperity, it was fashionable for richer people to move out of old family homes, and even to demolish them. Although a number of the surviving buildings are now being cherished and restored, some towns have been so changed that the character they had built up over centuries has been lost forever. Many cities of the Middle East bear scars from the speed of their development in the oil age. In Isfahan in Iran, for example, a grid of new roads was driven right through beautiful old buildings. Kuwait City, which had been a picturesque town up to the 1950s, was sliced up by six highways. Much of its core was bulldozed to make way for a

Sometimes a desire to seem modern has led to the demolition of handsome buildings that are part of the Middle East's heritage.

new central business district. It has now been recognized that hasty actions such as these showed little appreciation either of Islamic culture or of the practical advantages of the traditional Middle Eastern buildings for coping with the harsh climatic conditions.

International cities
Even where the old city centers have not been demolished, they are often now lost amid the sheer extent of the huge developments. With so much building going on in the last few decades, local styles have often been lost, and Middle Eastern cities have taken on an international appearance.

However, there are very few entirely new cities in the Middle East, despite the impact of oil.

In many Middle Eastern townscapes, only the occasional mosque among the international-style high- rise buildings may show what part of the world you are in. This is Cairo, with the Nile River in the foreground.

There is almost always a historic core somewhere within a modern Middle Eastern city. Unlike the international-looking developments around it, this core has characteristics that set it apart from the American or European traditions of city planning and building.

Islamic cities

A *medina*, or traditional Islamic city, generally had three elements: a citadel, a Friday mosque, and a market. The citadel was the center of government, and was often fortified. Sometimes, as at Aleppo in Syria, it was a full-scale castle set on a mound dominating the city. Although their fortifications are no longer needed, citadels are still sometimes used as government buildings because of their historical importance.

There are innumerable mosques in the lands of Islam, and many are small. The five-times-daily ritual prayers of the Muslim may be carried out anywhere, but every Friday the devotions should be shared in a congregation. A Friday mosque is thus a large one for communal prayers, and many mosques are famous for their size and beauty. They are sanctuaries of calm and meditation, in marked contrast to the bustle of the traditional trading area, and market.

Whether the market is called *suq* in Arabic, *bazaar* in Persian, or *charsi* in Turkish, it is a place of enormous activity. It is not just a place for wholesale and retail trading. A great deal of small-scale manufacturing goes on as well, with each of the similar trades and crafts grouped together. Thus sellers of nails or ropes will cluster together, and so will dyers and printers of fabric.

Bazaars are places where things are made as well as sold.

The alley where spice sellers are crowded can be recognized by its smell. The metal-working quarter, with its copperbeaters and blacksmiths busy over their anvils, can be identified by the noise. There is the gleam of gold from the jewelry quarter, and the squalling of loudspeakers on stalls where cassettes of local pop music are sold.

The modern bazaars of the Middle East are a strange mixture. Mass-produced plastic imports from Taiwan are sold alongside unique local products of ancient handicrafts. For example, lute building and carpet knotting use skills that are now difficult to find elsewhere in the world.

Town dwellers

The Middle East saw the emergence of some of the world's earliest cities. People were living organized urban lives in Mesopotamia and along the Nile more than 5,000 years ago. Today, about half of the population lives in towns or cities. While this proportion is still less than that of the

How Long People Can Expect to Live
In many Middle Eastern countries, only one person in 50 is over the age of 65.

In the past, the average age to which people survived was little more than 30, but people born recently have life expectancies that are closer to those of people in the developed nations. There is still, however, room for improvement.

Life expectancy at birth, in years

U.S.	73
U.K.	73
U.S.S.R.	70
Kuwait	69
Iraq	55
Egypt	54
Saudi Arabia	53
U.A. Emirates	47
Qatar	47

The streets of Middle Eastern cities are usually crowded and bustling, but families value privacy in their home lives. Often, town houses have few windows at ground level and these are tightly shuttered. Secure doors like these mark a firm division between home life and the noisy world outside.

world's advanced industrial nations, it is more than many developing countries. For example, only around a quarter of China's people live in cities, and in India little more than a fifth do. The lowest figures in the Middle East are in places like Oman and the Yemen PDR. However, in Lebanon and Israel, with their emphasis on trade and heavily mechanized agriculture, more than three-quarters of the people live in towns. The great majority of people are also town dwellers in the Gulf states of Kuwait, Qatar, Bahrain, Saudi Arabia, and the United Arab Emirates. These are all desert countries where there is little land for people to farm.

The very rapid growth of urban populations in the last few decades occurred not only because people moved in from the countryside. It also reflects rapid growth within the cities themselves, where much of the health care is now. Middle Eastern cities used to be notoriously insanitary and disease-ridden. Even up to the nineteenth century, hundreds of people died in epidemics of plague, typhoid, and cholera, and few people survived until old age. The number of old people in the population is still quite small. However, with improved health care, people can expect to live much longer. What is more, oil money means that at least some of the Middle Eastern cities make many cities in America and Europe look run-down and shabby.

11   Education, Work, and Oil

There are now a great many young people throughout the Middle East, because of the rapid improvement in health and welfare. Two out of every five people in most countries in the region are under the age of 15, and in some countries half the population is under 15 years old.

In some ways this produces problems. For example, when you deduct the number of old people no longer able to work, only about half of the rest of the population are grown-ups of working age. The remainder are children who have to be supported. The sheer number of young people is making it difficult to ensure that they get adequate education for the future. Recently, in Jordan, there were 27,000 applicants for just 3,000 university places in one year.

In Islamic countries, education has always been considered important. The Prophet is believed to have said that a father can give his child nothing more valuable than a good education. However, modernization has brought conflicts. Many Middle Eastern countries wish to shape education so that traditional Islamic values and lifestyles are preserved.

Educating women

Throughout most of the Middle East, there is a difference in the education for boys and girls. In general, more men than women have been taught to read and write, except in Lebanon, Cyprus,

The fact that so many of the people in the Middle East are very young makes it difficult to know how things may turn out for them in the future. Given the right chances these young people would clearly achieve a lot, but the countries of the area face great practical problems in providing education and jobs for them.

Israel and, to a lesser extent, Egypt. There are also great practical problems in bringing education to the people, particularly in the rural areas of the poorer countries. In the Yemen Arab Republic, for example, only one in 50 women over the age of ten can read and write. In village communities, some heads of families still believe that primary

In many parts of the Middle East, people in the country districts still live very much as they have for many hundreds of years. They may have transistor radios and be in touch with world news, but they still live in a very traditional style. Many villages have never been visited by a doctor, midwife, or dentist.

school education is enough for girls.

Most of the rich Arab countries are eager for women to have equal education. There are many distinguished universities in the Middle East, but bringing women into them presents problems in the stricter Islamic communities. When a woman does obtain a degree, it can be difficult for her to use her training. Some conservative families expect women to return to a traditional home-centered lifestyle when they have completed college. This is so even in countries such as Syria, where the most widely accepted Sunni form of

Islam is dominant. Even where women are permitted to become professionals, the community may feel that this should be done on a segregated basis. For example, in Saudi Arabia, where the strict version of Islam known as Wahhabism is practiced, it is not the custom for women to work with men, even though they are fully qualified. In their first years at school, girls and boys are taught together and play together, but later they are separated.

Sharing a school

Now that there are so many young people, there are not enough schools to educate everyone. In most countries in the Middle East, children must start school at the age of seven. Even with crowded classes of 50 to 60 children, it is often necessary to work a shift system. This allows the same set of school buildings to be used for twice as many children. The first group comes from 7 a.m. until around midday, and the second group comes in the afternoon.

The shortage of teachers is more difficult to solve. Egypt, Turkey, and Syria started to develop modern educational systems well before Saudi Arabia and the Gulf states began to invest their oil money in education. These late-developing countries have had to rely heavily on bringing in trained teachers from other countries.

Jobs abroad

Egypt supplies many teachers, doctors, and engineers to the whole Arab world, as well as semiskilled workers. In some years, two million Egyptians are out of the country, working mainly in the major oil-producing states. The money they send home makes a big contribution to the Egyptian economy. Yet, with a population that is expected to rise to 60 million by the year 2000, it is difficult for the Egyptians to decide whether that money really makes up for losing skills that are needed at home.

Migrating workers is also a difficult matter for other Middle Eastern countries. The fact that Arabic is a common language for so many of the countries in the region encourages people of all levels of education, from surgeons to laborers, to migrate across borders in search of work. Although many of the countries have very little or no oil wealth, all are affected by the well-paid jobs that are available in the oil-rich countries. Sometimes the effects are complicated. For example, Jordan is a poor country, and at times almost half its workforce has been working abroad. This has meant that tens of thousands of immigrant workers, mainly Egyptians, have gone there to replace Jordanians who have left.

In the oil-rich states themselves, immigrant workers can often outnumber the local workforce. This can be true even in as large a country as Saudi Arabia. It is even more apparent in the small Gulf states such as Kuwait, where immigrants make up two-thirds of the workforce. In Qatar and the United Arab Emirates, eight or even nine out of ten workers are from elsewhere. It is a source of great concern to local people to find that they are being outnumbered in their own country.

Most of the migrant workers come from other countries within the Middle East. However, around one in five are South Asians, particularly from India and Pakistan, though some come from as far as Korea, China, and the Philippines. Although their jobs are financed ultimately by oil money, most of these workers are employed in construction and service industries. The number working with oil itself is very much smaller, and such specialists are still often from the United States and Europe. Some migration has gone the other way. Several million Turks worked for a time in Western Europe, but they too are now beginning to turn to the oil-rich Gulf states.

Metals and other resources

There are certainly many other resources in the Middle East besides oil. However, these have a lesser influence on the way patterns of life in the

Although high technology industries are increasingly being introduced in the Middle East, many of the existing industries are based on traditional products. Here, wool is being dyed for carpet makers in Iran. The methods may be simple, but the final handmade Persian carpets are very valuable.

area are developing. These resources range from phosphates and brown coal to ores. They include iron and copper as well as rarer metals such as antimony, but none of them produces more than a few percent of the world's total. Nor is the

---

Industry in the Middle East

One way of judging the importance of industry in different countries is to look at what they export. What proportion of the export is manufactured goods as opposed to unprocessed agricultural products or raw materials such as unrefined oil?

In the Middle East, exports of manufactured goods have been most important in recent years to Israel and Turkey, representing well over 60 percent of their total exports by value. These goods range from textiles and processed foods from agriculture to chemicals and metal goods from mineral resources.

Manufactured exports are less important but still of value to Jordan, Egypt, and Syria, being respectively 50 percent, 25 percent, and 12.5 percent of their exports by value. Unprocessed agricultural exports are important for Turkey, Egypt, Jordan, Syria, and Iran.

In the main oil-producing states, less effort has usually been put into developing manufacturing. The sheer amount of oil they export dominates their economies. In Saudi Arabia, Iraq, Qatar, Oman, and the United Arab Emirates, unrefined petroleum has formed more than 90 percent of their exports by value in recent years. Even refined petrochemical products come a long way behind this, except for Bahrain where they form 80 percent of the exports.

Middle East one of the world's great manufacturing areas. Many of the industries there are based on processing local agricultural products, both foods and fibers, such as cotton and wool for textiles. Egypt and Turkey have had the longest experience in developing their industries. In the Persian Gulf states modern manufacturing has only been introduced since the 1960s, after the oil money started to flow.

Not all countries in the Middle East are interested in developing manufacturing industries. Some of the main oil-producing states around the Gulf have only small labor forces and few natural resources other than oil from which to make things. They prefer to develop their influence in international trading and finance. In Egypt, Turkey, and Iraq, with their larger

Turkey and Egypt are the Middle Eastern countries with the longest established modern industries, and both now have air pollution problems. Here, the minarets of Cairo fade into the industrial haze.

workforces and a range of other resources, industry may be the key to development.

Depending on oil

All the countries of the Middle East, even those with large oil reserves, are trying hard to reduce their dependence on oil. One reason for this is that every time that world oil prices fall the whole area is affected, directly or indirectly. This is so not only for the major oil producers themselves, but for the other Middle Eastern countries as well, because they are all so closely linked.

Another reason is that even countries with plenty of oil have problems in guaranteeing the continuation of their income. If the oil producers set prices too high, their customers will make greater use of coal or nuclear power, or will be more willing to develop difficult oil fields like those of Alaska or the North Sea. The Saudis have usually taken a very moderate line in oil price negotiations for this reason.

The most important reason for developing other forms of income is the fact that oil and natural gas reserves are being used up fast and can never be replaced. Some countries had little oil to start with, and for them it will run out very soon. The oilfields are spread unevenly within the Middle East. Most of the important ones are concentrated in an area of about 500 by 745 miles (800 by 1,200 kilometers) around the head of the Gulf. Saudi Arabia, Kuwait, Iran, and Iraq between them hold roughly 80 percent of the region's reserves, and many of the other Middle Eastern countries have little or no oil at all.

The oil in the Middle East represents about 60

How Long Can the Oil Last?
There is a lot of guesswork in assessing how long oil reserves may last. To start with, it depends on how demand may change through the years, and on whether new oilfields are discovered. The effectiveness of new techniques for getting more oil out of known fields is also important. Nevertheless, although the figures are only estimates, they show how differently these countries must view their future.

	Years from 1990 until oil runs out
Kuwait	271
Saudi Arabia	127
Abu Dhabi	94
Iraq	79
Iran	55
Qatar	23
Oman	15
Egypt	8
Dubai	6

Geologists suspect that there may be anywhere from 10 to 24 billion tons of oil still to be located in the Middle East—almost all in Saudi Arabia, Iran, and Iraq. This is not allowed for in the table, which is based on proven reserves at the production level of the mid-1980s.

percent of the whole world's proven oil reserves. "Proven" means that geologists have been able to make thorough checks on how much is available. Saudi Arabia's Ghawar field is the largest in the world, and it alone has twice as much oil as the entire proven reserves of the United States.

Although the Middle East is such a major producer of oil, it is not a major consumer. This means that it can sell most of its production to North America, Japan, and Western Europe, giving the area great importance in the eyes of the world. However, the rich variety of other things that the Middle East has contributed to cultures elsewhere in the world through the centuries should not be forgotten.

This strange-looking "bird" is actually a pump or "donkey" for an oil well in Saudi Arabia, the largest producer of oil. Oil is usually piped from the oil wells to the coast, where it is shipped abroad.

12   The Legacies of the Middle East

When people think of the Middle East, they think first of oil, because it is now so important in everyday life. However, even things as basic as the type of farming practiced in places as far flung as the United States and Australia started in the Middle East. Many other kinds of ideas have also come out of the Middle East besides ones about practical matters like food production. Several religions that have spread across the globe originated in the region.

In their long history of trading, the Middle Eastern peoples have provided other regions with goods, including specialities such as Persian and Turkish carpets, and have also acted as intermediaries. They passed on to Europe exotic products from the Orient, such as spices, and were supplying Chinese silks as long ago as Roman times.

Music

Although Middle Eastern and Western music have developed along rather different lines, many Western musical instruments have evolved from ones that first came from the Middle East. The idea of military bands first came from the Muslims and was adopted by the Crusaders. Individual instruments were also taken back to the courts of Europe. Sometimes the original forms of instruments now used in orchestras in the West are still played by Middle Eastern folk

The astrolabe was first developed in the Middle East to measure the height of the stars. European sailors used it for navigation in the great voyages of discovery of the fifteenth and sixteenth centuries, including Columbus's voyages to America. This is a modern one, made for use by astrologers.

musicians. The *zurna*, for example, is the ancestor of the oboe. Sometimes the Arabic names were adopted. Thus, lute comes from *al'Oud*, guitar from *qitara*, and the dance Saraband from *zarabanda*.

A more subtle influence of Middle Eastern cultures has been on Western language, which has inherited many everyday words from Middle Eastern languages. There can be annoying problems getting through the busy city *traffic* on the way to a shopping *bazaar*. Purchases there might include a *magazine*, or *rice*, *oranges*, *lemons*, *apricots*, *artichokes*, *spinach*, and even a *jar* of *syrup*. At the cloth counter *gauze* may be found, *muslin*, so called because it was originally from Mosul in

Al'Oud, *the Middle Eastern instrument from which the European lute was developed. This one has just been finished in the suq (bazaar) of Aleppo. It is inlaid with mother-of-pearl.*

91

Iraq, and *damask* from Damascus in Syria. A *mattress* could be covered with *cotton*, or a *sofa* with *satin*. The *tariff* could be paid by *check*. Shoppers then go home to collapse on the *divan* in the *alcove*, with a *carafe* of mint *julep*. Women might get ready for a party by putting on *mascara*. That might be a mistake, because the Arabic *maskhara* doesn't mean make up, but a buffoon or clown—the painted people!

Games

Western sports and games also show Middle Eastern influence. Horse racing is known as "the sport of kings"; it is also the sport of sheiks. Nowadays, some of the most important racehorse owners and breeders in the world are Arab sheiks. However, this is nothing new. Some of the greatest thoroughbred racehorse lines of the United States, England, and Australia started with eighteenth-century Arab stallions. The Middle Eastern influence on games goes back much further than that. Viking chessmen carved from walrus tusks have been found on the island of Lewis in Scotland, and it is known that chess came to the Norsemen through the Middle East. Chess players all over the world still call the move that finishes a game "checkmate." This is from *sheik maat*, Arabic for "the sheik is dead."

Export of ideas

The Middle Eastern heritage has been spread by contacts made through conflict as well as through peaceful trading. The Crusaders took some Middle Eastern ideas home to Europe. Arab conquerors held Spain for Islam for many centuries, and their legacy can still be heard in flamenco music and seen there in architecture. For example, there is the great mosque of Cordoba, which stands in a valley called Guadal-quivir by the Spanish, though that is really the Arabic *wadi al kebir*, meaning "big valley."

In the Renaissance, Europe rediscovered the heritage of the ancient world of Greece and Rome

Islamic metalwork is famous. Often the designs include sayings from the Koran in flowing Arabic lettering.

in science, mathematics, and medicine. This had been preserved by the Persians and Arabs. They had not merely saved it, but had also carried the knowledge forward in a way still valued by modern scientists. The Middle East has influenced the arts as well. Islam does not permit images of people in religious art, so Muslim artists have specialized in subtle geometrical patterns. The way they have used these in architecture, textiles, and metalwork has been admired and imitated by artists in many other parts of the world.

Both in large matters and in small ones, there is much more variety to Middle Eastern physical and human geography than is often recognized. Although its oil is extremely important, the rest of the world has inherited a great deal more than this from the diverse peoples of the Middle East.

Index

3/19
15
2/22
©1991